W9-CXX-725

Mel Bay's
BASIC BLUES HARP
by Phil Duncan

1 2 3 4 5 6 7 8 9 0

Visit us on the Web at www.melbay.com – E-mail us at email@melbay.com

TABLE OF CONTENTS

INTRODUCTION

You will need a 10-hole diatonic harmonica in the key of C. The letter C is usually stamped on the mouthpiece or the covers of the harmonica.

How to Read Arrows and Numbers

1. When the arrow is pointing down, it is DRAW! (SUCK)
2. When the arrow is pointing up it is BLOW!
3. The numbers tell which hole to blow or draw. The 10-hole has numbers on the top cover plate.

Single Tone
(Lip Blocking)

Pursing, puckering like sipping something hot and whistling, describes the embouchure (mouth position). This technique for playing is lip blocking. The tongue is usually back in the mouth not touching the mouthpiece. The lips are pursed, making the lips taller than wider. It may be necessary to move the harmonica to the right or left while you are creating an air stream so as to target one single hole.

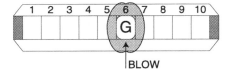

Vibrato

You may use your hands to change the sound of your playing by adding a wavering tone. Holding the harmonic in the left hand, close and open the right hand over the left. This will create a wavering tone while playing. Mov the right hand slowly for a rich, mellow vibrato or quickly to and fro to increase the vibrato. Some players use air to create a vibrato. Using small puffs of air when exhaling or inhaling into the harmonica will create a vibrato. Kee the puffs of air steady and increase the speed as you learn.

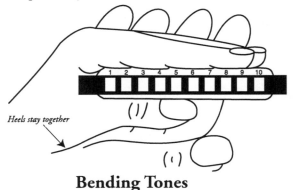

Heels stay together

Bending Tones

Bending tones, making the pitch (tone) lower is possible by slowing the speed of the vibrating reed. This is done b adding pressure to the chamber and the reed. Lip muscles need to be strengthened, therefore persistence will b necessary. It is suggested that you use a lower-pitched harmonica such as an "A" or B♭" harmonica. While drawing sucking air through one of the first 6 holes, drop your jaw, arch your tongue, and jet the air to the bottom of you mouth. Try hole one first. Once you hear the drop in pitch in hole 1, move to hole 6, followed by hole 4 and the hole 3 (this will bend further than the other holes) and lastly hole 2.

Blues Harp
(Cross-harp)

Second position, cross-harp, blues harp, blues harmonicas are titles used for playing blues. You play melodies using holes 1 to 6 and 6 to 10. This divides the harmonica into lower and upper sections. Hole 2, draw; hole 6, blow; and hole 9, blow are the main tones. This allows a 7th flat scale between holes 2 and 6 and between 6 and 9. The 7th flat tone is a "blues" sound. Using a C harmonica, you will actually play in the key of G. The "F" natural in holes 5, draw and 9, draw create the blues sound.

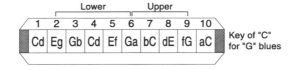

We use a "C" harmonica to play in the key of G. The following chart illustrates the blues harp/cross harp to use for each key.

Actual Harp	Cross-Harp	Actual Harp	Cross-Harp
C harp	G blues	F harp	C blues
G harp	D blues	B♭ harp	F blues
D harp	A blues	E♭ harp	B♭ blues
A harp	E blues	A♭ harp	E♭ blues
E harp	B blues	D♭ harp	A♭ blues
B harp	F♯ G♭ blues	F♯ G♭ harp	D♭ blues

BEGINNING BLUES PROGRESSION II

Phil Duncan

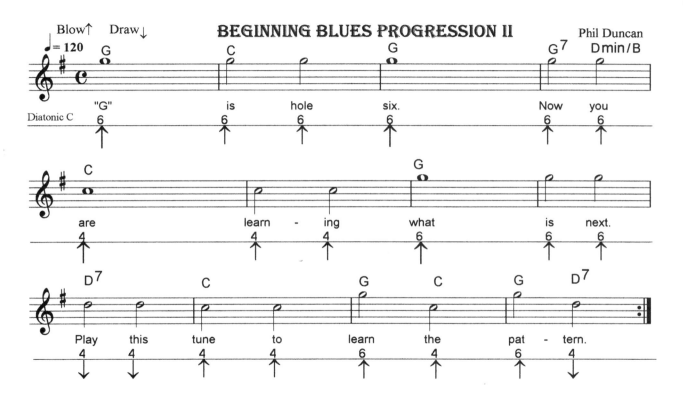

EASY BLUES

Phil Duncan

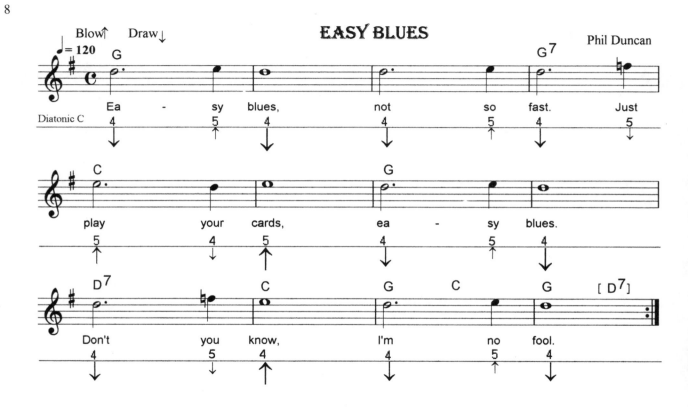

BEWARE BLUES

Phil Duncan

COMBINATION BLUES

Phil Duncan

COMBO BLUES

Phil Duncan

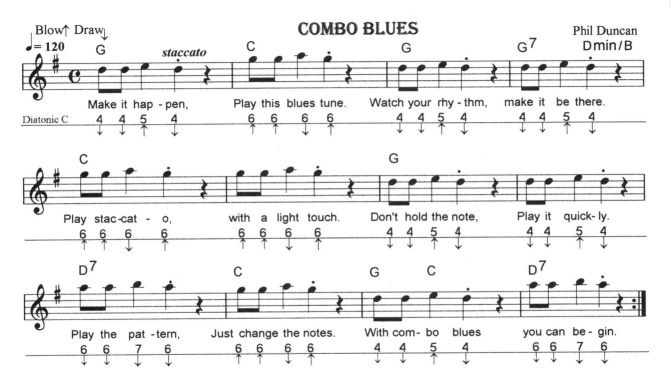

BOUNCE BLUES

Phil Duncan

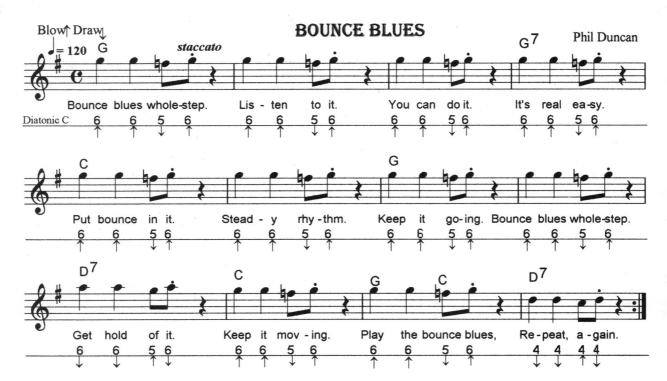

PUSHY BLUES

Phil Duncan

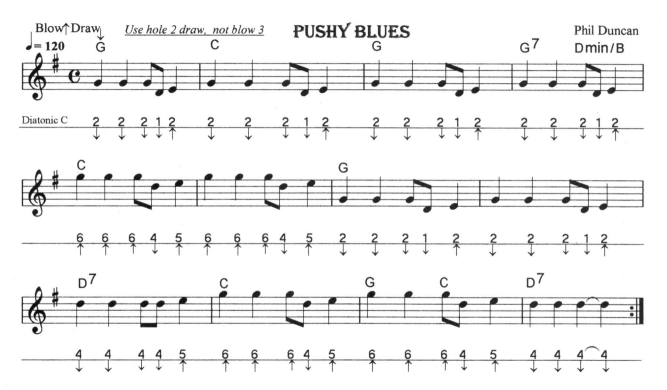

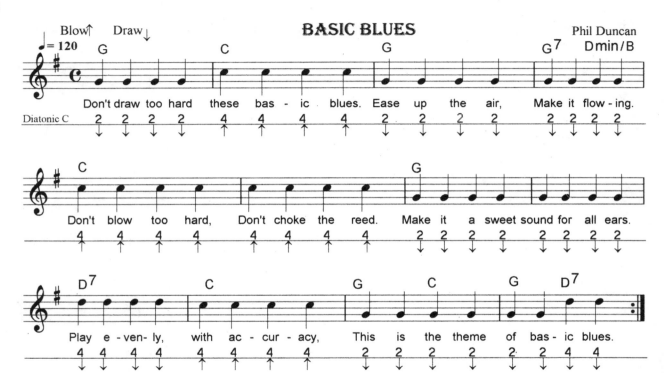

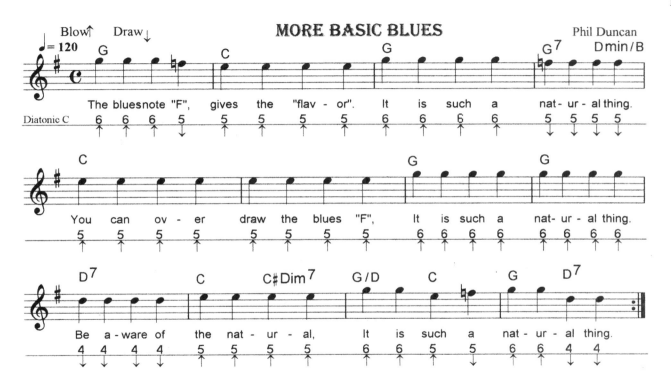

WALKING BOOGIE

Phil Duncan

BOOGIE ON DOWN

Phil Duncan

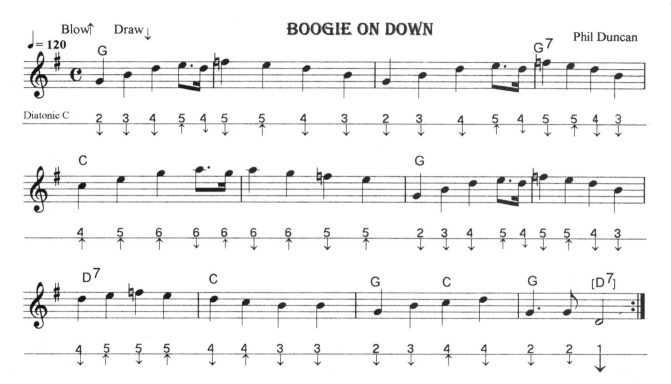

HARMONICA SHUFFLE

Phil Duncan

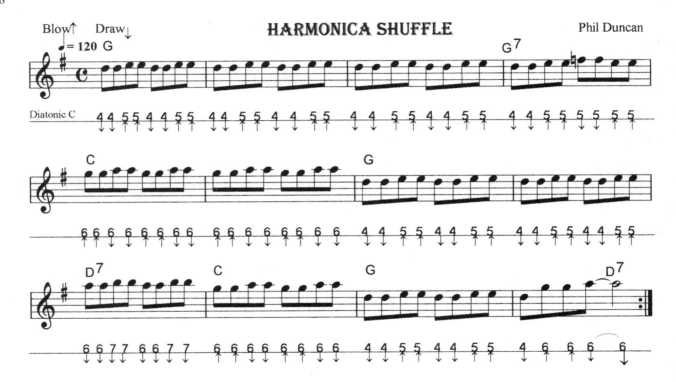

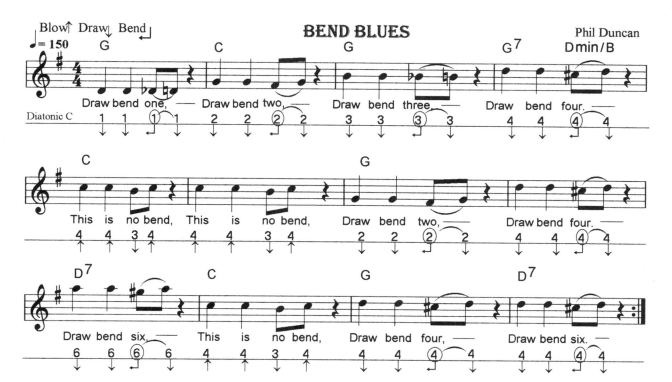

COME ON BLUES

Phil Duncan

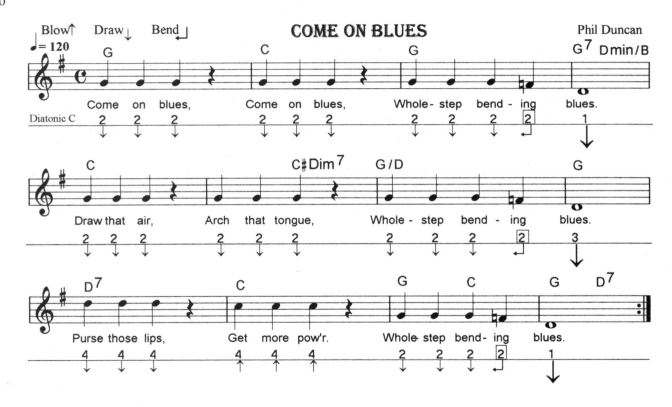

PICKUP BLUES

Phil Duncan

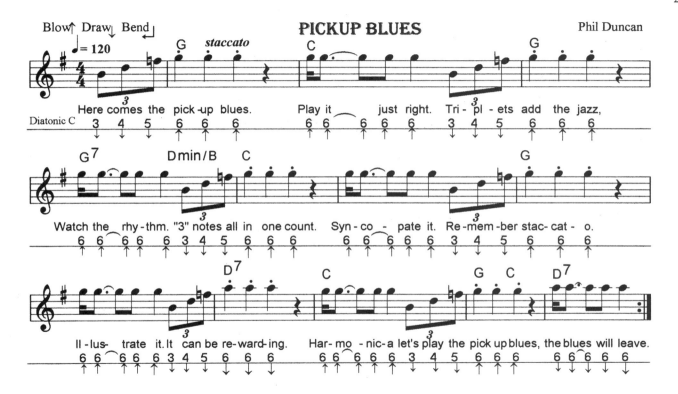

STOMPING BLUES

Phil Duncan

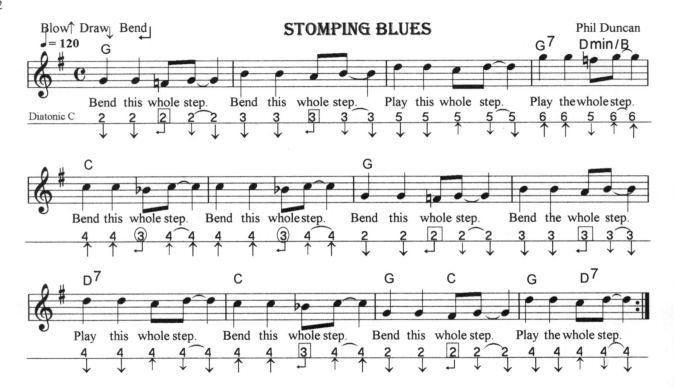

TARGET BLUES

Phil Duncan

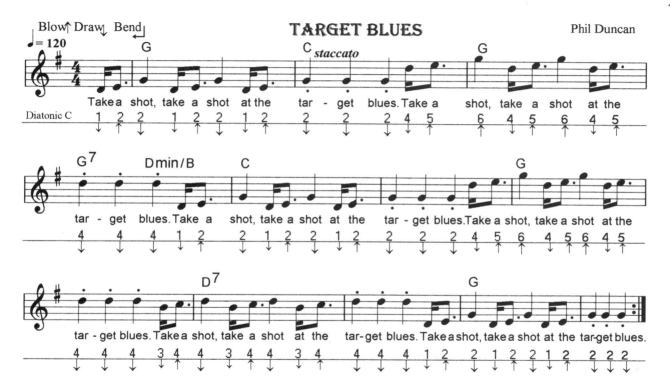

EASY ON BLUES

Phil Duncan

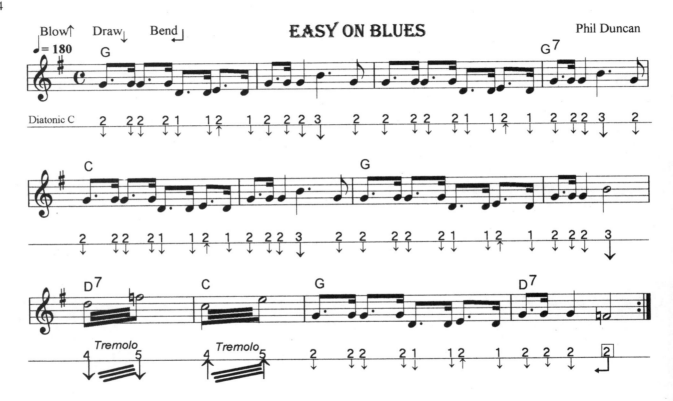

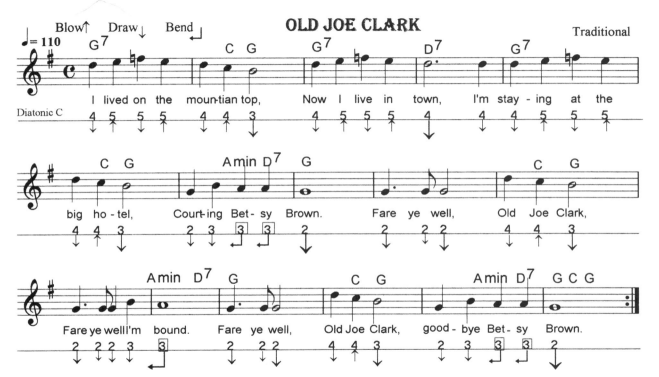

WHEN THE SAINTS

Arr: Phil Duncan
Traditional

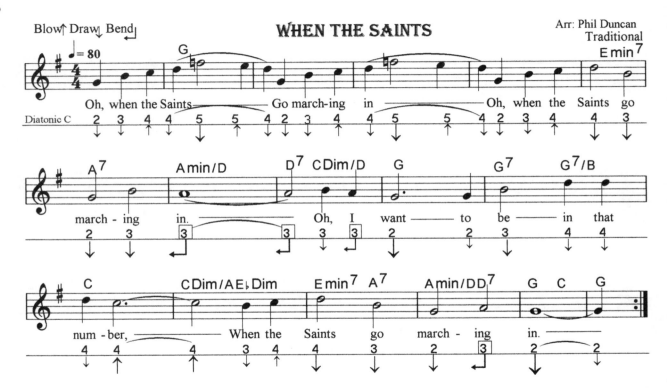

AMAGING GRACE

Arr: Phil Duncan
Traditional

WORRIED MAN BLUES

Arr: Phil Duncan
Traditional

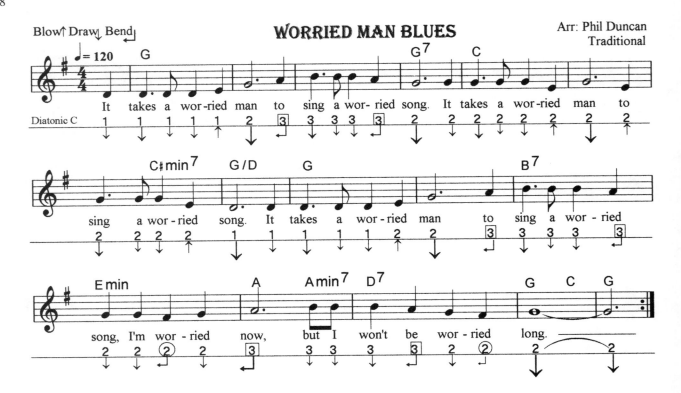

THIS TRAIN

Traditional

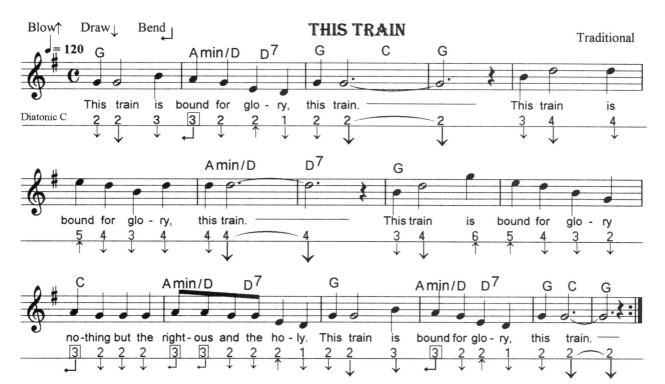

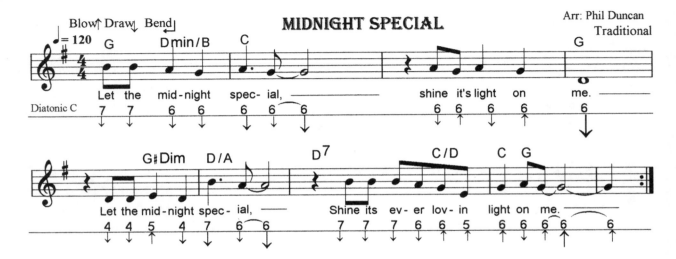

STANDING IN THE NEED OF PRAYER

LONESOME ROAD BLUES

Arr: Phil Duncan
Traditional